YAN-KIT SO

Chinese

Photography by SIMON WHEELER

THE MASTER CHEFS

TED SMART

YAN-KIT SO was born in China and grew up in Hong Kong. She settled in London in the early 1970s, and has also lived in the United States, India and France. She has given demonstrations at The Women's Institute and taught at notable cookery schools such as Leith's School of Food and Wine and the Cordon Bleu Cookery School in London.

Yan-kit So has written a handful of books on Chinese food and culture, including *Wok Cookbook* (1985), *Classic Food of China* (1992) and *Yan-Kit's Classic Chinese Cookbook* (1984), which won the two premier British awards for cookbooks: the Glenfiddich Food Book of the Year and the André Simon Award.

CONTENTS

Appetite

for food

and sex

is nature.

GAOZI (KAO TZU),
A CHINESE SAGE WHO LIVED
IN THE 4TH CENTURY BC
MENCIUS
(PENGUIN CLASSICS, 1970)
translated by D C Lau

INTRODUCTION

Chinese cuisine is accessible and versatile: it can be achieved with almost any ingredient from land or sea. The intriguing Chinese flavours are, more often than not, based on no more than salt, soy sauce, other soy bean products such as fermented black beans, sugar, vinegar and a little rice wine. Add to these the kitchen trinity of ginger, garlic and spring onion and the most popular spices, star anise and Sichuan peppercorns, and you are all set to cook Chinese.

While other cooking methods are used, unique is the technique of stir-frying which, in lightning fashion, turns morsels of ingredients in a wok into an aromatic dish full of flavours and textures, both crisp and succulent. Six of the recipes I have chosen are stir-fries: two are suitable for vegetarians, chicken has universal appeal, and the beef with oyster sauce is one of my favourite dishes. Monkfish is an amazingly good partner for black bean sauce and as for the prawns, they are so Chinese, so delectable, that I can never cook enough of them for my family and friends!

To create a meal for four to six people, choose one meat, one seafood and one vegetable dish from this book and serve with plain boiled rice. Don't forget that all Chinese dishes are meant to be shared.

BRAISED AUBERGINE
with pork

675 G/1½ LB AUBERGINES, TOPPED
    AND TAILED

SALT

4 TABLESPOONS PEANUT OR CORN
    OIL

2–3 LARGE GARLIC CLOVES,
    ROUGHLY CHOPPED

4 SPRING ONIONS, CUT INTO
    5 CM/2 INCH SECTIONS, WHITE
    AND GREEN PARTS SEPARATED

125 G/4 OZ PORK, MINCED

1 TABLESPOON SHAOXING WINE
    OR MEDIUM-DRY SHERRY

½ TEASPOON POTATO OR TAPIOCA
    FLOUR

1 TABLESPOON THICK OR DARK SOY
    SAUCE

¼ TEASPOON SUGAR

85 ML/3 FL OZ CHICKEN OR VEAL
    STOCK

SERVES 6

Cut the aubergines into pieces about 5 cm/2 inches long and 2.5 cm/1 inch wide and thick. Sprinkle 1 teaspoon salt over the flesh and leave for 1 hour. Rinse and dry thoroughly.

In a large, heavy-bottomed saucepan, heat 2 tablespoons of the oil. Add half the aubergine pieces and brown over medium heat for about 2 minutes. Remove to a dish. Add 1 more tablespoon of the oil and brown the remaining aubergine. Remove to the dish.

Add the remaining oil to the pan. Add the garlic and white spring onions, stir, then add the pork and stir vigorously until it turns opaque. Splash in the wine or sherry, stirring as it sizzles. Sprinkle over the flour and stir to coat. Reduce the heat slightly, add the soy sauce, sugar and stock and bring to a simmer. Return the aubergine to the pan, cover and simmer gently for 10–15 minutes or until meltingly tender.

Add the green spring onions, then taste and season. Transfer to a serving dish and serve hot.

SAUTÉED AND BRAISED COD

2 LARGE COD STEAKS, EACH ABOUT
275 G/10 OZ AND
2.5 CM/1 INCH THICK
1–1½ TEASPOONS CORNFLOUR
4 TABLESPOONS PEANUT OR CORN
OIL
2 LARGE GARLIC CLOVES, CRUSHED
1 TABLESPOON SHAOXING WINE
OR MEDIUM-DRY SHERRY
2 TEASPOONS FINELY CHOPPED
GARLIC
4 TEASPOONS FINELY CHOPPED
FRESH GINGER
6–8 SPRING ONIONS, CUT INTO
SMALL ROUNDS, WHITE AND
GREEN PARTS SEPARATED

FOR THE SAUCE
½ TEASPOON SALT
2½ TABLESPOONS THIN OR LIGHT
SOY SAUCE
1½ TEASPOONS SUGAR
8 TURNS OF THE PEPPERMILL
2½ TABLESPOONS UNSALTED
CHICKEN STOCK

SERVES 2-4

Pat the cod steaks dry and sift the cornflour over them to coat both sides of the fish.

To make the sauce, stir all the ingredients together in a small bowl until the sugar dissolves.

Heat a wok over high heat until smoke rises. Add the oil and swirl it around. Add the crushed garlic, fry until lightly browned, then discard.

Add the cod steaks and brown for about 20 seconds on each side. Splash in the wine or sherry; as the sizzling subsides, remove the wok from the heat. Spread the chopped garlic, ginger and white spring onions on top of the fish. Pour in the sauce.

Place the wok over medium heat to bring the sauce to a simmer. Cover and cook for about 4 minutes or until the fish is just done – a fork or chopstick will easily pierce the flesh. Spread the green spring onions over the fish and spoon some hot sauce over them. Transfer to a serving dish and serve hot.

STIR-FRIED PRAWNS
with pine nuts

450 G/1 LB UNCOOKED PRAWNS, IN
    THEIR SHELLS BUT WITHOUT
    HEADS (25–40 PRAWNS)
4 TABLESPOONS PEANUT OR CORN
    OIL
4–5 LARGE GARLIC CLOVES, FINELY
    CHOPPED
2–3 TEASPOONS CHILLI OIL OR
    CHILLI SAUCE
2–3 TEASPOONS THIN OR LIGHT
    SOY SAUCE
½ TEASPOON CORNFLOUR
    DISSOLVED IN 2½ TABLESPOONS
    CHICKEN STOCK
25–50 G/1–2 OZ PINE NUTS
SMALL BUNCH OF CORIANDER
    LEAVES (WITHOUT MAIN STALKS)

FOR THE MARINADE
¼–⅓ TEASPOON SALT
1 TEASPOON CORNFLOUR
1 TABLESPOON EGG WHITE

SERVES 4

Shell the prawns and devein by slitting along the back with a small sharp knife.

To marinate, place the prawns in a bowl, add the salt, cornflour and egg white and stir vigorously in one direction for about 30 seconds. Leave in the refrigerator, covered, for 2–3 hours or overnight. (This will help to seal the prawns in a crisp coating during stir-frying.)

Heat a wok over high heat until smoke rises. Add the oil and swirl it around. Add the garlic, stir for a few seconds, then add the prawns. Using a wok spatula, turn and toss for about 20 seconds; the prawns will curl and turn opaque. Reduce the heat to medium, add the chilli oil or chilli sauce and soy sauce and stir for about 1 minute.

Stir the cornflour in the chicken stock and add to the wok, stirring as it thickens. The prawns should be cooked by now. Add the pine nuts and stir to mix. Transfer to a serving dish, scatter the coriander leaves on top and serve at once.

BEEF WITH OYSTER SAUCE

225 G/8 OZ TRIMMED BEEF
(RIBEYE, RUMP, SKIRT OR FILLET
STEAK), CUT INTO SLIVERS
ABOUT 4 x 1 CM/1½ x ½ INCH
AND 5 MM/¼ INCH THICK
4½ TABLESPOONS PEANUT OR
CORN OIL
125 G/4 OZ SHIITAKE MUSHROOMS,
TRIMMED AND CUT INTO STRIPS
SALT
2 LARGE GARLIC CLOVES, FINELY
CHOPPED
4–6 THIN SLICES OF FRESH GINGER
3 LARGE SPRING ONIONS, CUT
INTO 4 CM/1½ INCH SECTIONS,
WHITE AND GREEN PARTS
SEPARATED
1 TABLESPOON SHAOXING WINE
OR MEDIUM-DRY SHERRY
1–1½ TABLESPOONS OYSTER SAUCE

FOR THE MARINADE
¼ TEASPOON SALT
1 TEASPOON THICK OR DARK SOY
SAUCE
6 TURNS OF THE PEPPERMILL
1 TEASPOON SHAOXING WINE
OR MEDIUM-DRY SHERRY
1 TEASPOON POTATO OR TAPIOCA
FLOUR
2 TEASPOONS SESAME OIL

SERVES 2

To marinate, place the beef in a bowl, add the salt, soy sauce, pepper, wine and flour and stir in one direction until well coated. (This coating will help to seal in the juices during stir-frying.) Gradually add 1–1½ tablespoons water, stirring vigorously until absorbed. Stir in the sesame oil.

Heat 1½ tablespoons of the oil in a frying pan over medium heat and fry the mushrooms for 2–3 minutes, adding a good pinch of salt. Set aside.

Heat a wok over high heat until smoke rises. Add the remaining oil and swirl it around. Add the garlic, ginger and white spring onions and stir to mix. Add the beef and, using a wok spatula, turn and toss for about 20 seconds or until the beef is partially cooked. Splash in the wine or sherry, stirring as it sizzles. Add 2 tablespoons water and reduce the heat, stirring as the water is incorporated. Add the mushrooms, green spring onions and oyster sauce, stir to mix, then transfer to a serving dish and serve at once.

BRAISED DUCK
in spiced soy sauce

1 DUCKLING, ABOUT 2 KG/4½ LB,
   OIL SACS DISCARDED, SKIN
   PRICKED ALL OVER
85 G/3 FL OZ PERNOD OR CHINESE
   MEI KUEI LIEW WINE

SPICED SOY SAUCE
375 ML/12 FL OZ THICK OR DARK
   SOY SAUCE
2 LITRES/3½ PINTS WATER
125 G/4 OZ CHINESE CRYSTAL OR
   DEMERARA SUGAR
1 TABLESPOON SEA SALT
25 G/1 OZ FRESH GINGER, BRUISED
1 WHOLE OR 3 PIECES DRIED
   TANGERINE PEEL
2½ STAR ANISE PODS
5 CM/2 INCH CINNAMON STICK,
   BROKEN UP
1 TEASPOON BLACK PEPPERCORNS
2 TEASPOONS SICHUAN
   PEPPERCORNS
1 TABLESPOON FENNEL SEEDS
1 TEASPOON CLOVES

GARLIC DIPPING SAUCE
4 TEASPOONS VERY FINELY
   CHOPPED GARLIC
6 TABLESPOONS WINE VINEGAR OR
   CHINESE RICE VINEGAR

SERVES 6
Preheat the oven to 240°C/475°F/
Gas Mark 9.

Put the soy sauce, water, sugar,
salt, ginger and tangerine peel in a
large, heavy-bottomed saucepan.
Tie the star anise, cinnamon,
peppercorns, fennel seeds and
cloves in a large piece of muslin
and add to the pan. Slowly bring
to the boil, then cover and simmer
gently for 30 minutes.

Meanwhile, fill a roasting pan
with about 2.5 cm/1 inch of water
and place the duck on a rack over
the water. Roast in the hot oven
for 20–25 minutes; this will rid the
skin of much of its fat.

Bring the spiced sauce to the
boil, add the Pernod or wine and
let it bubble for a few seconds. Add
the duck, breast side up, cover and
simmer very gently for 30 minutes.
Remove from the heat, turn the
duck breast side down and leave in
the sauce, covered, for 1 hour.

For the dipping sauce, mix
together the garlic and vinegar.

Carve the duck. Strain the
spiced soy sauce and serve as an
alternative dipping sauce.

STIR-FRIED MONKFISH
with black bean sauce

500 G/1 LB 2 OZ MONKFISH FILLET

1½ TEASPOONS CORNFLOUR MIXED
WITH ¼ TEASPOON SALT

2½ TABLESPOONS FERMENTED
BLACK BEANS, RINSED

¼ TEASPOON SUGAR

2 TABLESPOONS SESAME OIL

3½–4 TABLESPOONS PEANUT OR
CORN OIL

1 TABLESPOON FINELY CHOPPED
GARLIC

1 LONG FRESH RED CHILLI,
SEEDED AND CUT INTO ROUNDS
(OPTIONAL)

1 TABLESPOON SHAOXING WINE
OR MEDIUM-DRY SHERRY

¾ TEASPOON CORNFLOUR
DISSOLVED IN 3 TABLESPOONS
CHICKEN STOCK

ABOUT 12 LETTUCE LEAVES

SERVES 4

Pat the fish dry and cut into pieces about 2 cm/¾ inch wide, removing any membrane. Coat evenly with the seasoned cornflour. (This will help to seal in the juices during stir-frying.)

Using a spoon, mash the fermented black beans with the sugar and sesame oil to form a coarse paste.

Heat a wok over high heat until smoke rises. Add the peanut oil and swirl it around. Add the garlic, chilli (if using) and black bean paste and stir to mix. Add the fish, turn and toss for about 30 seconds or until browned on all sides. Splash in the wine or sherry; as the sizzling subsides, reduce the heat and continue to stir-fry for about 2 minutes or until the fish is cooked.

Stir the cornflour in the chicken stock and add to the wok, stirring as it thickens. Transfer to a serving dish and arrange the lettuce leaves around the edge. Serve at once.

STIR-FRIED CHICKEN
with mangetouts

325 G/12 OZ SKINLESS, BONELESS
CHICKEN BREAST FILLET, CUT
CROSSWAYS INTO THIN SLIVERS
SALT
5 TABLESPOONS PEANUT OIL
175 G/6 OZ MANGETOUTS OR
SUGAR SNAP PEAS, TRIMMED
2 LARGE GARLIC CLOVES, CUT INTO
THIN SLIVERS
4 LARGE SPRING ONIONS, CUT
INTO 4 CM/1½ INCH SECTIONS,
WHITE AND GREEN PARTS
SEPARATED
1 TABLESPOON SHAOXING WINE
OR MEDIUM-DRY SHERRY
1 TEASPOON CORNFLOUR
DISSOLVED IN 4 TABLESPOONS
CHICKEN STOCK
2–3 TEASPOONS SESAME OIL

FOR THE MARINADE
½ TEASPOON SALT
¼ TEASPOON SUGAR
2–3 TEASPOONS THIN OR LIGHT
SOY SAUCE
1 TEASPOON SHAOXING WINE
OR MEDIUM-DRY SHERRY
8 TURNS OF THE PEPPERMILL
1 TEASPOON CORNFLOUR
1 TABLESPOON EGG WHITE
1 TABLESPOON PEANUT OIL

SERVES 4

Put the chicken in a bowl, add the marinade ingredients and stir until coated. Leave for 15–20 minutes.

Bring a saucepan of salted water to the boil and add 1 tablespoon of the oil. Blanch the mangetouts for 10 seconds or sugar snap peas for 1 minute after the water returns to the boil. Drain in a colander, refresh with cold water and leave to drain.

Heat a wok over high heat until smoke rises. Add the remaining oil and swirl it around. Add the garlic and white spring onions and stir to mix. Add the marinated chicken and turn and toss, using a wok spatula, for 30–40 seconds or until the chicken is pale all over. Splash in the wine or sherry, stirring as it sizzles; reduce the heat.

Stir the cornflour in the stock and add to the wok, stirring as it thickens. When the chicken is cooked, add the mangetouts or sugar snaps and green spring onions and stir until everything is hot. Transfer to a serving dish, drizzle with sesame oil, serve hot.

STIR-FRIED CHINESE LEAF
with oyster mushrooms

1 HEAD OF CHINESE LEAVES, ABOUT
    600–675 G/1¼–1½ LB
150–175 G/5–6 OZ OYSTER
    MUSHROOMS
4 TABLESPOONS PEANUT OR CORN
    OIL
6 SLICES OF FRESH GINGER, PEELED
4 LARGE SPRING ONIONS, CUT
    INTO 4 CM/1½ INCH SECTIONS,
    WHITE AND GREEN PARTS
    SEPARATED
¾–1 TEASPOON SALT
1½–1¾ TABLESPOONS WINE
    VINEGAR OR CHINESE RICE
    VINEGAR

SERVES 2–3 VEGETARIANS, 4–6 WITH OTHER DISHES

Separate the Chinese leaves and rinse the outer ones to remove any dirt. Cut the leaves in half lengthways, then cut crossways into 5 cm/2 inch sections, separating the stalks and leafy parts. Set aside.

Cut the oyster mushrooms lengthways into strips.

Heat a wok over high heat until smoke rises. Add the oil and swirl it around. Add the ginger, stir, add the white spring onions and stir for a few seconds. Add the reserved stalks, turn and toss vigorously for a few seconds.

Reduce the heat to medium. Add the salt, which will draw out moisture from the Chinese leaves. Add the vinegar, stir, add the oyster mushrooms, stir, then add the leafy parts. Continue to stir and cook for about 5 minutes, depending on how crisp you like the Chinese leaves. Add the green spring onions, stir to mix, then transfer to a serving dish. Serve hot.

STIR-FRIED BEANSPROUTS
with courgettes

3–4 TABLESPOONS PEANUT OR
    CORN OIL

1½–2 TABLESPOONS SHREDDED
    FRESH GINGER

400 G/14 OZ BEANSPROUTS

400 G/14 OZ COURGETTES, TOPPED
    AND TAILED, THEN CUT INTO
    THIN STICKS ABOUT 5 CM/
    2 INCHES LONG

½ TEASPOON SALT

2–3 TEASPOONS THIN OR LIGHT
    SOY SAUCE

1 TABLESPOON SESAME OIL

SERVES 3–4 VEGETARIANS, 6 WITH OTHER DISHES

Heat a wok over high heat until smoke rises. Add the oil and swirl it around. Add the ginger and let it sizzle for a few seconds. Add the beansprouts and courgettes, season with the salt and turn and toss vigorously until the beansprouts begin to release their water.

Add the soy sauce and continue to stir and turn for about 5 minutes, varying the heat between high and medium, until most of the moisture has evaporated. Add the sesame oil and transfer the mixture to a serving dish. Serve at once.

FLAVOURED GLUTINOUS RICE

500 G/1 LB 2 OZ THAI GLUTINOUS
RICE, RINSED THEN SOAKED IN
5 CM/2 INCHES OF COLD WATER
FOR AT LEAST 4 HOURS
5 TABLESPOONS PEANUT OR CORN
OIL
4 LARGE SPRING ONIONS, CUT
INTO SMALL ROUNDS
40 G/1½ OZ DRIED SHRIMPS,
RINSED, SOAKED IN JUST
ENOUGH WATER TO COVER FOR
1 HOUR, THEN DRAINED
25 G/1 OZ CHINESE DRIED BLACK
MUSHROOMS, RINSED, SOAKED IN
300 ML/½ PINT HOT WATER FOR
2–3 HOURS, DRAINED THEN
DICED
325 G/12 OZ LEAN BACON, FRIED
THEN DICED
LARGE BUNCH OF CORIANDER
LEAVES (WITHOUT MAIN STALKS)
SALT
SOY SAUCE

SERVES 3-4

Drain the rice, then stir in 1
tablespoon of the oil. Smear 1
tablespoon oil over a perforated
steamer container with fine holes
and spread the rice over it. (If the
holes are too large, cover them
with muslin.) Cover and steam
over boiling water for 30–40
minutes or until the rice is cooked.

Heat a wok over high heat
until smoke rises. Add the
remaining oil and swirl it around.
Add the spring onions, stir, then
add the dried shrimps and the
diced mushrooms and stir until
piping hot. Remove from the heat
and add the hot sticky rice; mix
well, breaking up any lumps. Mix
in the bacon and the coriander
leaves. Taste and add salt and soy
sauce if required. Serve hot.

This can be prepared in advance.
To reheat, add 1 tablespoon oil to a
warm wok and spread the rice
mixture over the base. Place over
medium-low heat until the bottom
has formed a crisp crust. Turn the
mixture and toast the other side,
adding a little more oil if necessary.

THE BASICS

INGREDIENTS

SOY SAUCE

Made from fermented soy beans, this ancient Chinese invention, now used all over the world, is the indispensable seasoning of Chinese cuisine. Often used in conjunction with salt, the two main kinds of soy sauce are the dark or thick, which is less salty in taste, thicker in consistency and adds its dark colour to the dishes in which it is used, and the thin or light, which is more salty in taste but does not colour the food. Soy sauces can also be used in marinades or as dipping sauces.

OILS

For most stir-frying and other cooking, use a neutral-flavoured oil such as peanut or corn oil. Sesame oil is very aromatic and strongly flavoured; Chinese sesame oil is processed from roasted white sesame seeds, and the cold-pressed Middle Eastern sesame oil should not be used as a substitute. Chilli oil (sometimes labelled chilli hot oil) is also strongly flavoured; there is often a sediment in the oil consisting of chilli, dried shrimps, garlic, vinegar, salt and sugar. Stir the oil and sediment just before using it.

WINE

Shaoxing wine is named after Shaoxing (sometimes spelt Shaohsing), a small town near Shanghai. It is fermented from glutinous rice and is amber-coloured and fairly dry. A clear Chinese rice wine or medium-dry sherry can be used instead. Mei Kuei Liew wine is more often used for cooking than for drinking; it is a strong liqueur made from sorghum and flavoured with rose petals.

RICE VINEGAR
Chinese rice vinegar is less sweet than Japanese rice vinegar – its acidity is more akin to white wine vinegar. It is clear, and is used in cooking and pickling vegetables.

GLUTINOUS RICE
This is also called sticky rice because the grains stick together when cooked. It is often associated with Thai cooking.

OYSTER SAUCE
This is a southern Chinese sauce made from extract of oysters. It adds a meaty, savoury-sweet taste to food; its brown colour comes from caramel.

DRIED ORANGE OR TANGERINE PEEL
This adds a subtle orange flavour to braised Chinese dishes, and is often used in conjunction with star anise and Sichuan peppercorns. The dark brown, brittle peel can be bought in Chinese supermarkets, or you can make your own by leaving pieces of clementine peel in a dry, airy place or on a sunny windowsill until brittle. Soak in cold water until pliable before use.

STAR ANISE
A perfect star anise is a hard, reddish brown pod with eight segments, each containing seeds. Aromatic, with a liquorice flavour, it is used in braised poultry and meat dishes.

SICHUAN PEPPERCORNS
Less burning hot than black peppercorns, these reddish-brown dried berries from western China have a slightly cooling, numbing effect on the palate.

FERMENTED BLACK BEANS
Whole soy beans, fermented and preserved in salt and ginger; on their own, they have a tangy and slightly bitter flavour, but when combined with garlic in hot oil, they become black bean sauce, which is used in many dishes.

CHINESE CRYSTAL SUGAR

Also called rock sugar because it comes in lumps of different sizes, it is pale yellowish-brown in colour and is often used in spiced soy sauce or in sweet 'soup' desserts.

DRIED SHRIMPS

These are shrimps which have been preserved by peeling, salting and drying. They are used as a seasoning for vegetables and in stuffings.

DRIED MUSHROOMS

Dried shiitake mushrooms are almost black in colour; they add their flavour to the dish in which they are cooked, but also absorb other flavours. Soak in warm water until pliable before use.

CHINESE LEAF

This is a type of cabbage with pale leaves which form a long, compact head. It is sometimes known as Chinese celery cabbage and its official name is *Brassica chinensis*.

EQUIPMENT

A wok is the ideal piece of cooking equipment for stir-frying and many other cooking techniques. A generous-sized sauté pan, allowing room for vigorous stirring and turning, can be used instead.

A wok spatula has a rounded end to match the base of wok; this allows efficient stir-frying.

It is a good idea to warm your serving dishes before adding the food, especially stir-fried dishes, because they tend to cool very quickly.

THE MASTER CHEFS

SOUPS
ARABELLA BOXER

MEZE, TAPAS AND ANTIPASTI
AGLAIA KREMEZI

PASTA SAUCES
GORDON RAMSAY

RISOTTO
MICHELE SCICOLONE

SALADS
CLARE CONNERY

MEDITERRANEAN
ANTONY WORRALL THOMPSON

VEGETABLES
PAUL GAYLER

LUNCHES
ALASTAIR LITTLE

COOKING FOR TWO
RICHARD OLNEY

FISH
RICK STEIN

CHICKEN
BRUNO LOUBET

SUPPERS
VALENTINA HARRIS

THE MAIN COURSE
ROGER VERGÉ

ROASTS
JANEEN SARLIN

WILD FOOD
ROWLEY LEIGH

PACIFIC
JILL DUPLEIX

CURRIES
PAT CHAPMAN

HOT AND SPICY
PAUL AND JEANNE RANKIN

THAI
JACKI PASSMORE

CHINESE
YAN-KIT SO

VEGETARIAN
KAREN LEE

DESSERTS
MICHEL ROUX

CAKES
CAROLE WALTER

COOKIES
ELINOR KLIVANS

THE MASTER CHEFS

This edition produced for The Book People Ltd,

Hall Wood Avenue, Haydock, St Helens WAII 9UL

Text © copyright 1996 Yan-kit So

Yan-kit So has asserted her right to be
identified as the Author of this Work.

Photographs © copyright 1996 Simon Wheeler

First published in 1996 by

WEIDENFELD & NICOLSON

THE ORION PUBLISHING GROUP

ORION HOUSE

5 UPPER ST MARTIN'S LANE

LONDON WC2H 9EA

British Library Cataloguing-in-Publication data
A catalogue record for this book is available
from the British Library.

ISBN 0 297 83645 5

DESIGNED BY THE SENATE
EDITOR MAGGIE RAMSAY
FOOD STYLIST JOY DAVIES
ASSISTANT KATY HOLDER